# RANGE FINDER

## DAVID PERRY

★

ADVENTURES IN POETRY

Some of these poems appeared previously
in *Sal Mimeo* and *Insurance*.

Cover: "Studio Table I" 1999, by Trevor Winkfield,
courtesy Tibor de Nagy Gallery.

Special thanks to Lisa Corson.

ADVENTURES IN POETRY titles are distributed
through Zephyr Press by
Consortium Book Sales and Distribution
www.cbsd.com
&
SPD: Small Press Distribution
www.spdbooks.org

9 8 7 6 5 4 3 2 FIRST PRINTING

ADVENTURES IN POETRY

NEW YORK          BOSTON

WWW.ADVENTURESINPOETRY.COM

ISBN 0-9706250-2-2

# CONTENTS

# RANGE FINDER

# URBAN POD ON A HILL

Far be it from me to fetch forth
A pill and in jest inject
Vitreous humor with light until
Aperture edges suddenly outwards

Yield sign against a field of winter wheat
Two men taking turns smacking a third
Rows of parked cars like fascicles
Whatever's before us comes in

Makes itself at home turning us into
Spectators of our own exasperation
Elation a dodge ball hurled well
Into the back with the *ponk* of the vanished

# Dark Matter

Perhaps it is to have an attack while at rest,
Rather?  Sudden thunder under the sun

Or to allow one to come over
As if at will or even in peace, as if

Naturally?  It would seem
To be in us to do so.

Darker still the mind,
As years of soot on stone

Or snow on the road
Make forms too large to see.

Black ice in the lake at night.
We may yet have it up to here

Where the head is all body
And doubt the whole of belief.

## Range Finder

I have nowhere to go that isn't
automatically written language.
People will talk and sometimes
I will listen, or so I say. Yet what is
there . . . nothing but suddenly
this wrung language, that flooded
engine, this gusting room of ghost notes?
The dead set receives the wantoning
of spring by summer and fall.
How it does that I do not know but

find upon release from my person
by moonlight that I too am beautiful,
less memory than memory-less,
a contentment seldom known outside
of childhood. I'm on my very own
great plain, alone among lawn jockeys,
heat lightning and unbidden sightings,
switching back against countless blades.
Are we dressing for dinner? Yes.
Out here things run clear yet

fine lines like electric fences articulate
where *like* operates in the open to keep
things apart by design of some kind
of superthing. As with words, all points

point outward in a mad dash to vanish.
I'm left to my thoughts and the thrill
of *ad nauseum*, punching big holes in
myself with pleasure to let the oceans out.
Or at least a seagull. *As is* is as *as does*
enough to keep everybody being.

Unsudden clouds mob the bad moon
and every moment lists in everything
now appearing: my particle world
where it all happens. Here there
are shapes I thought to be important
before I was enameled by things
and shellacked into position. I am
a beautiful handicraft finished in late
Missouri light by artisans manqué.
Here's what I've picked up as a puppet:

You're not just human, rather more
or less, depending, and you're not
just being, you're also some other
ing, existing *in situ*, instead of this
institution, or not at all, in place
of nothing. Much is intuitive, like
the compulsion to fake it for real,
or how vertigo lets you know how
high you really are when you channel
a bird that drops because you can't fly.

Or how we slip into each other's
streams and there's not a fair fight in all
the best places. O Particle! The inanimate
soul objects, but doesn't listen and can't
answer. I miss the pathetic fallacies of table
talk, pillow talk, a kind ear, an open heart.
I liken some things/unliken others
with a few words, yet other things—alien/alike—
zither through my nervous system, in orbit
about the shifting zenith beneath my lids.

# REPLICA

The sun is one you know—
Another last turn to go

Until you're done being here
But not yet begun elsewhere

We don't get it like this often
Enough to trace its descent

Dueling all through the house
And out into the street below

The window of your most recent
Reflection appears without a dent

Two rights and a left to the liquor store
Mysterious premonition of rapid turnover

Enough! Between us is a fence
With you, object of frustration

Consciousness cut in two or more
Lots to be re-divided later

Words want us to do things
That we can't do with them

## Shin Bark

The problem is everything we know
Say your name to yourself until your
Voice becomes that of another person
Repeated until it's of another thing
Is how my tongue became an anther
Why bees come to sting me numb

Epistemologically speaking with
A lisp an impediment a murker
Of sense there is the lightning
Beetle alighting while cicadas thrum
Through their thoraxes in deep dusk
The moment of sleep before sleep

If you wake up someone else
You can only hope that someone else
Will wake you up and call you honey
Rule of thumb where we come from
If you can't touch it without thought
Feelings as sap will certainly follow

The willows bow to the lawn
Water until the drought comes
Then our sophistication siphons
The rest out of some unseen forest
Where we do not hear the clear cut
Or feel the crushing of our tongues

## Aubade

What glazes the sky
Burns the eye
And poses come over the animals
As in every mating season

It's good to be gone again
Stuck on some *pièce de résistance*
In a reclamation area
By the recently adopted stream
As the cold spell of election
Touches down to lay waste
Outside the comfort station

      \*

The highway's a loop
Though it never returns
Us to this spot

For a second
You're the one
Thing that matters

*

The weather is something else
Silvering the interior

Feelings are light at first
Like our medium the air

*


The hare on the hill
The fish in the stream
The Storm King in the mist
Sit quietly

A nice spot for surveillance
Our minds have been changed
In much the same way
I will go to the machine for ice

# NOW WE ARE SIX

The last thing I recall from childhood
Is a hook-and-eye rug unraveling
One thread around my thumb tighter and thicker
A bulbous-tipped purpling spool of myself
On my awkward way downstairs
To wrack and ruin, death-in-sleep, circling the airport
So many ways to go it would seem
Not to mention the sea with its water
My grandfather was a Pall Mall interior punctuator
Arguing sluices and locks with phantom engineers
Of his own maledictions
Weighed down with great wings
Amidst the rapture and the lust thing
He wrote a very good poem about a very bad mope
He found himself mired in it
And it coalesced about his head like gelatin
Why can't you settle down and make beautiful love
Like the magazines below decks
I'm going to write you a prescription
For something called "early retirement"
My mother is a beautiful beluga
Perhaps you've heard her supersonic song
In your subaquatic dreams
The good doctor is in reality a deadly asteroid
He winked at me from inside his funny plush purple animal outfit

They called him "Grimace"
Somehow they slipped me his dreams
Of grapples with angry fish and fiery cetaceans
Slinking up and down my spine
Like a cloud of sixteen sibilants
Pierced with seventeen sweet whistles
Pluto dug me up
No different than a soup bone or missing fission rod
And my fathers before me
All of us seemingly subject to the whim
And wisdom of calmly cycling the service road
Then spring came
I whiled away and seethed
Like purling scud in the creek behind the house
Such were my sheets at that moment
Festooned about the bungalow's many mirrors
Gales of hard luck rattled the casements
My parents appeared in the bay window
Lit by the moon
In infinite recess
They reached their individual apogees
As a downpour smeared the area
Engulfing the silhouetted girders
Thus I recall my childhood
Fascination with archery
And rocketry capable of killing all conversation

# THUNK

The object of my failure is description.
A portrait of a ghost, like the one before you
waiting for you to catch up with it: your likeness
in the space where you keep appearing
and disappearing, knowing it will come again
to prime the brain with its many unstable compounds.

That's for time to know and space to find out
in the sunset of a former colonial outpost
or mournful site of lost imperial glory
giving one a sense that one does not
want: that of being there and nowhere in particular

where formative things (uptake inhibitors)
were meant to happen, and did, with the inevitable
mutations. Everything's been wired since
I awoke. Listen. Them's the boids!

## LISPED CUSSING

Intelligent death is never discussed
Thump among the trees

Emerging from the furniture
As our cells boil over

Slowly. Orgasm means the end
Of a perfect day or something.

I'm going home again to ask
For the key to the antique clock

And the remote that works
The satellites to turn the signals

Back on their sources in our heads.
Chips in the night air. Somewhere

In the distance I'm coming down
Getting up off the redwood deck

It's as if we start out broken
And meet in complete darkness.

# Circular No. 1

The light between the spheres has been stolen again. An inside job, no doubt, leaving somnambulant dummies rudderless in imitation of the domesticity favored by spent nomads. Hallucinations prowl the baseboards and molding, then flash into the open, never to see in themselves any sense except subliminally. To be perfectly frank, some of our best ideas never made it beyond pre-school.

This would seem disaster enough as is, but no, we must have more—cancellations, *trauerspielen*, days without breakfast, hodgepodge, awful haircuts.

Allow me to explain. Things that aren't here are almost always there, forming a perspective you call your own. I hesitate to draw you into this, but you are already implicated by dint of having woken up this morning with your knickers in a twist.

Without regard for those afflicted by our inborn predilection for pleasure, lines of force emanate from scrunched foreheads when we feel too hard or think too bad, creating net gains in pain. Most people are not interested—they may *say* otherwise, but never *are* otherwise. But the rest of us are exactly the same. Thinking about this for real would entail chasing, catching and letting go, yet what you chase is not what you catch any more than it is when you let it go. This is rote. It was here before and will come again. Little birds tell us how nice it is outside.

The last little bird seen was fluttering to death in the gutter. The cat watched from beneath the car.

Please think like the children. Where would *you* hide? In nature?

# FIFI

The people I know—
if only you knew them too
you'd be closer to me. Too close.
Where the air is hinged
light drips through the drapes,
fine hairs all around me
paving the way for night.
It's the only way I can experience life
I'm afraid. As for smoothness
I can't find the conjunction.
What's a missing poodle to do?
A keening in my ears,
cupcake fragments—that sort of thing.
In the end, life is unreconstructed
slush. Cats come in from the rain
to sit and wonder. Feed them.

But we must stop walking
at the speed of what we left behind.
Come on in and stack yourself in the corner.
Wait with me for winter to wind down.
You're my choice—for now.
Yes, the talking dog,
suspicious friend of man,
alone in the dark
waiting for the call in the woods
or the lights to come up.

## BLEEDER'S ROCK

It would only be a pleasant surprise
and in no discernible pattern
yet with the same thousand-yard stare. It hung
in space for a very long time, revolved
once, and disappeared. At least I think.
Or was it my radio alarm? Turns out
there's something to the questions burning
in everyone's minds. So I stay undercover
yet noticeably over the top. Which magic
button do you push, panic or snooze?
I seem to be on my way to work again.
For I *am* my work. Now you know.
Quite a puzzle, the breakout of walls
and walks growing from our brains
into the city with their ears and eyes.
They are human in ways unnatural—
how you say, *inhuman*. May I borrow
some of your light? Would you care
to have some air with me? It would be sweet.
But first the funhouse, then the tunnel,
then the bargained-for. What could people
possibly want with *that*? That's what I thought
yesterday when I got through with life—
as we know it—for the umpteenth time.

Wait, I take it back. The train appears
in the station. I notice I'm neither
on nor off. Everyone rises at once
like startled geese. Everyone else, that is.

## Pronoun Trouble

The tangles of newness confuse Louis XIV—shouldn't it be smoother? Who spilled their guts? Does anybody in these woods have a poker face for the sign of the times? Regardless, there they go again, making deposits without leaving their apartments.

This has been the case for years. The best question? *How could you?* Just ask the Archaic Torso. I did and still don't understand. Truth and Beauty turn round & round on the octopus ride. According to the accountants the gold came from the mouths of Congolese war dead.

Though we've already misplaced the car, fate provides perpetual motion, threading us through the crowd to where there's smoke. A pill delivers chit-chat via a system set to variations on, in and of repetition. Can we account for anything in a real moment? This brings me to the dilemma of all the other moments, and back again.

★

The age-old cry of *do over* doesn't stop the water from pooling in the sub-basement. Time withdraws and then envelops. It does it all, really (truth in deed separated from the doer). Our fantasy is control and what it does to us is just that. Few notice and even fewer care, down to the one or two who feel it and, like anything sensible, react.

Our world may be the sum of such reactions, making all things go at once. It's wonderful to be part of something. But as Louis now knows, that's just our world, the one in which we are gods the people have long since written off. No more imagination, rather impersonation populated by things beyond our control for a minute, until the ocular snaps. The bridge is out. So's the tunnel. Have you seen me do you? I do a good you.

## POLTERGUY

Well if I behaved like a child
when we were together he's
dead enough now, tearing down
curtains and knocking over
vases because it really hurt.
Sometimes he's beyond dead.
My life is garnished by a constant
rotating wreath slowly replacing
the shoes I don't like with ones I do.
Dressed, undressed. Askew brick walls
press bales of sunlight into wedges,
diving through splits in the city's bulk,
leaving all below luminous
like a star blanket or your palm
lit through by flashlight.
You were American to the last,
meaning you came first and left early.
You could afford to be interested but
uncommitted. There was distance on your side.
I was American, too, craving a transplant
after a life of self-abuse. Thus
we needed each other. Hey.
We're clumsy because we want to be.
A rope pulls around a corner
tied at one end to a towering cairn
of cobblestones, whatever is ready
for the heaping.

## Fifth or Sixth

Be gracious and accept
the armature of concourses
and culs-de-sac in the event
of a freak flash flood of feelings
(business *and* pleasure). At least
that's what I tell everybody. But I've never
told a soul what I'm about to tell you.
No, wait.... Ah, the tenor cuts loose
with his haunted-house riff. There's a spirit
that does not like it. They're hanging drywall.
Renovating for the new century won't likely
disturb our undead lifestyle, yet the old stories
get me to thinking: Move to the city center
where the horror blisters. Anything
to relieve the sensation of having a retired
hack on your neck. And you, flat
on your back. If this isn't manifesto enough,
you'll have to find other ways to scratch
the itch of loneliness. I know
you like the *idea* of sharing. Some final advice
before we take up our positions and congeal:
put your best foot forward in the manner of those
afflicted by acute *noblesse oblige*. "This will hurt
me more than it will hurt you" is a good one
to drop in advance of any movement.

## SAD WALK

Impoverished on the wing
If you have to *tell* the birds to sing

How curious the stillness
Rises to crush us!

Wouldn't you know sunshine
Comes in through experimental hoops?

Promontory socks the wind
Rushes of coming to after being out

And despite appearances such as ocean blue
We are not better off as people

# Why Am I So Nice?

First the need to revise arises from a desire to have needs beyond those shared with the rest of us. Sharing needs houses desire and yields pleasure at meeting or aching at thwarting to varying degrees, depending, in most respects, on the extent to which meeting relieves thwarting (eating, sex, sleep, shelter &c.). The second need to revise arises from the desire to live on—and off—excess: in, out, over, beyond, within, under, behind, above—exceeding that which is often perceived as "not bad," cool even. In extreme cases, basic needs may lose ground to a desire for something Edward G. Robinson called "more"; regardless of tendencies towards debilitating preoccupations with attainment of such, people seem able to accept shelter and, from time to time, take a bite of food. Finally, the mechanisms and channels through which pleasure might flow unimpeded come close to passing—and missing—those same people, though the summa of such sudden coursing *is* always available to the human sensorium. For example, I now realize how much of my popularity in high school was part and parcel of a complex schematic purportedly lost to fire. With respect to my formative social development, books were, to a great extent, responsible for mediating between two or more positions of power and penetrating the March of Time until all was revealed as empty space and light—somewhere, at least, to blow smoke and attend to the neglected needs of the last in line—or first, if reversibility of positions may be deemed permissible under such timorous circumstances (it may). Thus, the experience of meeting you here now seated before me could be my lucky break.

It's been years since we've had the luxury of spending a moment together, and I still wonder: What drove us apart? When I saw you in the audience, I immediately thought of alternate beginnings and modified middles, but no endings. Whichever way, that was one long moment. Funny thought, it comes out in a gush of truisms: You've changed, good to see you, it's been a while. I don't want to be taken for ventriloquist *or* dummy, just a nice guy—but not "nice" or "guy" in the accepted sense. So I mean what I say when I say: You look *good*.

As for the rest of you, I'd like to take the remaining time to break down some barriers (imagine abstract fields littered with chunks of concrete) in order to meet all the way. I thought we could begin with language and work our way up to child's play. Imagine taking my hand. Of course we're not going to *do* anything to make anyone uncomfortable. No accounting for the way we live, what we think, believe or let happen, with or without a peep. None of that, just a pleasant exercise in imagination, where the word "possible" shifts in its meaning ever so slightly.

Hey! I'm talking to *you*. Remember damming the creek with crud as it made its way to the beach? Remember our sunburns and the scratches on our arms and legs? Every touch became wonderful pain. You ran up to me under the pines among the ruins of the old borax plant as the hail began to pelt and you planted a big one full on my lips. We were such kids! You probably remember differently now, but you remembered differently then. The rest, as they say, is personal. I'm sure we'll meet again, and I'll see *you* after the performance. You can stop imagining now.

One parting thought. It's an odd world, old, and for that better felt than uttered: Rejoice.

# THE DAYS OF OUR LIVES

## *Julian Year*

Traps are cake to construct
From Tuesdays 'til paper maché
Alphabets hedged & sculpted
Powers get lonely in their abhorrence
Vacuums don't work or play
Floors worm through to ceilings
Or earth recedes into—what else?
Space limns time or etches rather
Bores through mathematics physically
As Lobachevsky did before he awoke
A dream about this guy who works
Behind a bar to support something


## *Fashionable Senescence*

Foil angels foil devils foil souls
Eternities blister & rise in the oven
They should be done by dusk or so
Your father's worst habit would indicate
A failure of definitions to allow love
The sun expands like indestructible robots
So does everything eventually come to think
Rooted in family roasted up right like Paradise
Indestructible roosters make cock fights a bore
Is it possible for these poor enjambed children

To find the tiny leg room needed for kicks
On a Friday or any last day before we forget


*Teriyaki Flamethrower*

Once upon a whim the calendar'd been
But alas no later than Wednesday last
Though braces never make young girls happy
Come right back & never leave this prejudice
Unrummaged but waiting forever
Get into her hair & you've made it
Some of them will come & worship Oh
Others won't come at all & will
Worship seeming or being maybe or probably
Not rapture or rupture with certainty
It's sad when kids start to read the *New Yorker*
No light comes in no light gets out


*Stop Me*

Yellow days don't last a day
Our Hero turns out to be this color
Between you & me is rather transparent
To the necktie striped bold & tight
Everything's blooming necks & eyes
Lightning on a Thursday all right
There waits the future in need
Of a good dressing or undressing

What has that to do with hats & why
Is Our Hero really just a version
Opposite Grant Wood's stoic stands a tree
Who knows modeling's pain better than a model


*Jokes Are All He Knows*

Acrylic black boa dragged through
The sands of an abandoned Canada
Our Hero turns out his collar
Is it frost then that's th' teeth o' the storm?
Though traces never made horses happy
Monday came this way says legend
There awaits the failure to add
Came right back & never left
Our Hero's head turns lavender
Get programmed i.e. with it
Tall boy or flight path you be
Straighten up a sudden breath of pepper


*Arbus Dubs*

I'm sorry I lost the treasure map
Swamp-combing the ex-drive-in
I ate the poisonous decoder cracker
So I'll be in the green room sighing
Lit by the cast iron pink grate smattering
Smeared with cayenne paste & wasabi

Or drowsing in a hot donkey cart
Sunday there's a lepidopterist pin party
In honor of a sexier science we all watch
Our compound eyed lying hearts crumple
Horror we look back & think OK OK
Cruelly seized by our cooling bones


*Old Lightning*

From his first words emerge his last
Will he or won't he do as we should
We are told by our progeny as jokes
Towering twists of lexica from many mouths
Everyone who ever mouthed mother darkens
Woe to the glasspipe & delicate antennae kids
He is clumsy & forgets to handwash
Fighting rust on a ragtop coupé
The horizon bloops into Saturday a lump
We all have one each of us has exactly one
Once it's gone it's no longer each of us
A boomeranged kangaroo biting the sawdust

## Ancestral Wig

The pleasure boats bumping along
By way of waves and particles

As though sketched in my daybook
Modeled on dusk and the old gray mule

Over the breakwater thoughts occurred
With the oncoming noxious fog

The tide dropped two feet in six seconds
To the surprise of all the sea creatures

For the pilgrims bumping along in their cars
The sun is the mind of God on drugs

While we made our way by foot through the fen
To confront at last what we most feared

And slipped away and walked the strand
To find everything just as it was

## Not Even Trying

What am I doing? Only writing my way into an apocalypse with what little physics I know. It's enough to keep most people at bay while letting the rest in for casual get-togethers leading to *stress* like the window cracked by the sky on your face at dawn. It's not what you might think, having been in school, but trust me. I like to climb trees. See? I get so sick of poetry *qua* you-know-what-I-mean the only thing that works anymore is letting the world get close, then reading to it. I don't care what words come, but I *am* aware. I powder my prose; I wish to keep it dry or dull, as in "flammable" or "dull roar," as in the earth beneath me holding up those on the other side, weather permitting, all the way to the Dogstar. Expanding universe: *go!* The main word is "full," which resonates with "empty."

## Extra Dawn

The last lesson of the season was don't forget
the end comes up through the earth like grass.
She turned toward the greenhouse
in the photograph. The sun wasn't lost
on the polished grain at her feet. Out on the lawn
the government went *bang*—or was it *bong*?
Worn wooden handles fastened with loose screws
to warped doors and peeled paint lakes and clouds.
Freedom on her head. Sometimes the missiles
rained from the sky, sometimes they hung around
the horizon. The first session
closed the book with a muffled *whump*.
Her finger was in it as her heart went
through the motions. She wore time out
at school and was sent home with a note.
"Powder keg" was her favorite concept.

Return to the day before once upon a time
was upon her. The wind whirled her skirts
as the sky emptied light into the sea.
Breakers brought news of the same
from the other side of the world.
Suddenly the others went along with a system
of sorting that left her cold. For a girl
who'd learned the language so fast she thought

she should be able to forget it just like that
but no. She felt a tug. Stop dreaming,
said the driver as he pulled the truck off the road.
Later she thought how small talk was
like fighting fake fights—a waste of breath
missing from people's faces as they showed
their teeth. All anyone seemed to see or say
had something to do with their stuff.
She sought truth in a town of cracked mugs.
But she had forgotten her lesson,
which everyone knew had something to do
with the end coming up through the earth like grass.
Nevertheless, she fought the real fight
with every word she withheld
and returned to her mind each night like a bat.

## Dear Obelisk,

what's wrong with you? I have some serious doubts. To be querulous seems to me the bean-curd of the matter, which may be the problem when it comes to commuting through red-blooded history or whatever they call our condition these days. I don't mean to be reductionist or rude, but you keep changing inscriptions, names, and addresses. When I say I want freedom, I don't mean *from* or *to*—I'm looking for another preposition entirely. The snap of the released, not by any means at your disposal, but tethered to my leg. No need to name it. Do they understand? They nod their conglomerate "yes," but their eyes are of another order. They do not suffer the little children so hot but rather snuff them with Ritalin and Smarties and pack them off to the future in crates. Did anyone get those invoice numbers? What do you mean by hiding under these ripening corpses? Listen, when the Mongols come cruising through, noggins will be lopped for sure—but don't blame it on the Mongols. If they hadn't returned to Mongolia for a funeral, all Christendom would have been martyred.

## After a Fashion

As we enter the tunnel the shrill whistle blows
Surprising us in our queries re the scheduled arrival
You have a nose for others but can't seem to find yourself
Coming out of the woodwork with sparks of fair warning
I'm having a hard time telling the truth
About the tracks being absorbed by the violet fog
All I can make out are fuzzy lines forming in my head
Leaning turns the train sharply but can tip it
In an instant where life just happens
We get tired of one car and wake up in another *ad infinitum*
I know it sounds crazy but I'm getting an *idea* about us
Negating the force of *somebody's* smothering effect
To keep getting it is one definition of addiction
You want to know what another is just ask

## A Flick of the Switch

I

I'll come down for food
At the end of the time change
If you haven't hurt anything new
I have islands in my bloodstream
And lungs like a kite
That say *do me* to the weather and tails
Snap in my mind long before
It happens in the sky

Here in the dim lounge
You are my sunspot
You don't refract or contract

I'll make a catapult
And together we'll lay seige
To the sleeping city
Afterwards maybe take in a movie

I have that feeling of suddenly being
In a zoo within a zoo within a zoo
Seeking some kind of sympathetic arrangement
Between the cages
*De*rangement is more like it
If only we could see each other
It would be like the future passing
Of days spent in active memory loss

Remember our plans?
Me neither

I can't dispel the wind
Without my walls
Though I recall certain
Cloud-gazing moments
And perfect bird calls
Hitting the right notes for hours
One long hello

Weather changes places
With an apple on the countertop
Which brings me back to you (and food)

Let there be eggs for all
I'll hatch them to perfection
Just wait until those chicks see the reign
Of benevolent light in their first days
Then experience one of those vodka sundowns


2

That oughta hold the little bastards
Teach them not so much to think
As sit around the dorm
In a fashion reductive and deadly
Like women powdering at the oasis
In the slant rays of heatseekers

Back when I was a kid
Things were otherwise known
As *out there* despite all the crap
Happening inside our own dirty number
The unlearned songs of Irving Cohen
Fading like the day you inside-outed me
At the den meeting and all the times
We missed each other on the couch
I got up and went straight to the terminal
Where a Pan figure announced a time change

Time out in this world of art installations & triumphal arches


### 3

Sometimes I think you are the creature
You said you felt you were
Apart from me so far
But soon to be by nature in the dark
Remembering is never enough

Packing boxes in the attic
I was thinking we *could* be together
With the chickens
But I took off
And everything was up in the air

Perhaps it was *your* vanishing act
The terrain favored it after the war

Or rather the absence thereof
Though it *did* happen but not to me
You were no trouble at all

We brought each other objects
As was the custom of our people
Paper that darkened when struck by light
Nuts berries collages and drugs

Or was it lightning striking at night
The suddenly life-size relief
Flashing on the real world of that time

But what *you* thought came back
And torched our barn with true compassion

# Notes on a Blown Notion

I'm glad I did what I did last night.
I could do it once again if only
over your dead body. And that, Jack,
is definitive fact. Count: (1) Police
chopper blocks moon, threshes
the dark through a large-guage
need for absolute power.
(2) The little grasses
sit suspect, each act
of congress in the grass between
us, as it were (and it were)
appears in sudden relief—syntax, say,
snapped everywhichway in the
hidden valley of our collected words.
(3) The afternoon's emotional cakewalk
in the park could have been around
an upset pedestal. Step down, please.
Be famous on your own time. Thanks
to the little people I no longer have
to make my story up (the one about the grass).
(4) I can sit back and let it
spin itself into
some abbreviated future.
Maybe that was the understood thing
mentioned in the hypnogogic almanac I found
stuffed in the old wicker hamper down in the basement.

(5) Consider the bin
as if it were an engine
in a flowerbed
filled with books
where one can dry out
one's brains.  (6) A slick surface,
a twitch in the eye. Will these hold together
without an audition?  I so long someday to be one
of the voices in your head, but only later,
after I've arrived.  I'm going over it now in the mirror.

## SCOTSMAN ON THE GREEN

The rustle of blue silk against a granite ledge.
Below, whistling tea kettles—
ancient science spun on its head.
The stars looked best from a great distance—
a bluff at dusk with spates of swifts
flushing mosquitoes from mackerel skies.

Grace notes from a Gatling gun
unhorsed the memory of our prank
as the brambled hardscrabble spread
surfaced, riddled with oil slicks.
Past the quicksand and thickets
of et ceteras & ampersands you'll find
the green. Our caddies will meet
all your needs, even a good long
golden pull on the string in your back.

## Sans-a-Belt Variations

Do you just do this and hope
things will do that? Can you trust
putting it in motion? The questions
coil in thickening club air. Darts
litter the linoleum
among dank jungle flowers
exuding the Waters of Forgetfulness.
An empty stretch of error extends
to old days unseen everywhere along
the way. But new things were perfect
then. That's the whiskey talking.
We have no excuses for our lost
findings, though surely we'll find some.

*Several weeks pass in advance.*

The answers came too late; we were all
volunteering at retirement communities,
doing some recon, hoping to squeeze
a good deed in sideways perhaps.
But time was such that we couldn't look
back and see anything—it was like trying
to take back a look. Or a breath. No fair
if by fair you mean a bunch of folk
having a great time together. Then
there's death, domain of fuel

for all those tomorrows and a way
to go that can't be recorked.

*Streams of passersby ago . . .*

The furtive "dang" of the dispossessed
is home, pulling cotton from the necks
of medicine bottles, checking late scores
on cable, evanescing like rumor among
the normal and the bored, who forgot already.
If you can purge yourself of the end . . .
This one thing comes up again and again.
There must be a point where you stop
and think.  But time is such
that you can't restart or finish.
Time for your nap?  No. The game's on
again and this time it's really big,
so get outta here already.

*Picking up from the previous fall . . .*

Everything seemed bigger. We settled
on buds freaked with orange
only to miss dawn again.  Dreams
condensed beneath lids then evaporated,
messages scrambled by bad connections.
Such loving touches wasted on details of appearance.
Are we enchanted enough to meet?

*For Your Eyes Only*

Stars collapse in the lobby,
fraudulent science comes true
at the vanishing point. You groped for your chair
and we drank the whole distance in
between us until the lights hit . . .
immediately—that's my memory.
Fidgeting while sitting still
was a major pastime then.
Hurry down the hall. I want
to get back in time to save the world
for later. They've put a fix
on the game and all we've got
to lose is consciousness.

# IN THE PARLANCE OF THE RUMMY DEAD

Unless I'm right I will go insane
In the radical sense of the word
Which is unknown for at the root
Some feel themselves wrongly *there*

This fatal mistake goes back a long way
Only to return with companion
But—& it's a big but—actual time
Can still be found whole in space

Other faces in light rotation
Come calling via antique vision rays
Who would live again given the chance
In the rented space of our vacant stares

★

I was at least twinned in my dream
You were there too in between
Suggesting without moving your lips
A check of the tombs for evidence

I could only smile the smile
Of the man who sold the Brooklyn Bridge
Or the boy who stole the honey bun
Nobody wants to hear about my dreams

If you will admit your ventriloquism
I will confess my *Dummheit*
There's nothing to lose that hasn't been
It is after all the future again

# THE BLACK ART OF PUNCTUATION

Any read read off the palm or
A ward of the state of the stars
Gives back more than it receives
In stares meant as secrets but open
To sneak breath on the neck

A rack of affection (drawing us
Across time—our lives
Thinning in the atmosphere
Beyond the storm) gives
The room back to the walls

In the cards the couple couple
In the cabinet the key to the closet
In the dark bowling ball
We were down before we got up
And that is the actual news

# Wonders of the Invisible World

"And refrigerate them crazy bones" said Carlos, passing me a wet ice pick. If not for his Byronic leap from cellar to willing doormat, I'd have considered his words the first stage of the parade I knew he'd been dreaming up. "For you to break apart that re-refrozen ice blob in the fridge." It was true: The sea rose in the desert, looked around and decided to settle; the moon was a tossed navy weather balloon at the apex of its arc. Just drive and find a parking lot anytime, anywhere. See, I figure Pangea lasted, oh, a million years, and that means it was *intentional*. Some people talk like it was a test or prototype of "today," but they don't even know the history of their own two hands. To get me angry, you just have to point them out—those same people walking around like they're some kind of helicopter gunship. It was a huge ball of ice, honeycombed like a hive of gigantic subzero bees. They'd be great on Europa or Pluto, or maybe the dark side of Mercury. It's too bad about common knowledge, how everyone who has it gets all worked up about it. If only they'd dwell awhile on the eternal return of tomorrow. *That* would be nice . . .

Back to the *soi-disant* parade. "Too bad whirlybirds aren't real. Birds, I mean." Sure, Carlos. The excruciating question of who will be the next knucklehead is keeping me on tenterhooks. Damn the development of film! (Outside, nobody even knows what that *means*, though the screen is attached and stretched like jersey). So we're all set to watch science switch from fiction and back to science—it's sort of hard *not* to, though the fog rising from the bog is all in our heads, making it hard to see. But who needs to see?

# THE ALIEN PRESENT

Come down to earth to write in the dirt
The planet needs you to flatten it

When not asleep or bored or ashamed
Of what we've seen and done nothing about

We try to put this thing back together
But so many answers come up questions

★

This is where the itch started
A brilliance in us that wasn't cast

By raising our antennae
A clicking in the tall grass

Everything is permitted
Tonnage chimes in the sky

★

The reluctance to stay
Became the fear of going

Though the circuit we formed
May break as more enter

With no feeling for things
Leaving us hanging like falls

# L

As soon as I write the call comes in
On impossibly close waves
The angle is also straight lines
Implying more or a mirror
Than a sidelong asymptote
Home can be a curve too
Appearances taken up in the air
With us against the world
Veering to meet upon the moment

## Before Things Get Better

The inherent possibility of us
being fashioned into think-pieces came in
last: blanks filled by more blanks.
What would our forebears of sense say
if put to the abstract? We came
to smirk and stayed to smile
but found some physical problems
too personal to share here in the sense
of knowing what we're talking about
without having to explain.
This is a trick of Mr. Chan and his sons.
Get ready for reversals of powerful—
what's the word? *Ching!* Such was our long-shot
fortune told by a tumbleweed.
Come to think of it, it blew away
long before we got to Needles.
But stay! It tumbles around
yet another gunky bus depot. Marvel
(and it *is* marvelous) or carefully knock
what you think to be your best luck
into the gulch. Try to loosen the fundament
without tipping it into your lap. Telepathy
is so messy. The sidewalk just came up
and attacked me. Where were we again?
All I want to know is what's going on
and if it's any good.

Typeset in Bembo.
Book design by *typeslowly*.
Printed by *McNaughton & Gunn*
in a first edition of 500 copies.